Shyloe and the Mayor

Doris Gaines Rapp, Ph.D.

Illustrated by - Doris Gaines Rapp, Ph.D.

Shyloe was six years old. She would start second grade the next day and she would be on time. She was almost always on time. That was very grown up.

Shyloe believed she should always be a good citizen. During summer break she and her little sister Sara went with Momma to the city parks to pick up trash and help keep the city clean. The girls saw little ground squirrels scamper through the bushes. They nibbled on any nuts they could find. Shyloe loved to watch them.

The summer was fun, but summer vacation was coming to an end. Shyloe was waiting for school to start. She was getting bored.

One late July afternoon Momma said, "Shyloe, why don't you make a poster? Don't be bored. You're a doer. Do something about trash. You could make a no-littering poster."

So Shyloe made a poster and titled it, Don't Trash on Your Future. She told her mother the words she wanted to have on it, and Momma wrote it for her, like a secretary. Then Shyloe decorated it with stickers of trees and colorful butterflies. The sticker glue was a surprise to Shyloe. It made the trees smell like evergreen pine.

First, Shyloe put the poster in her bedroom window so people driving by and walking past could see it. One day she said, "Momma, no one can see my poster. Please, put it up in town."

Her mother opened her eyes wide. "We would need permission to put up a poster in town." Shyloe looked out the window toward the stores downtown. Happy banners and signs hung from tables at the Farmers' Market in the next block where people sold sweet tomatoes and apples.

Shyloe asked her momma, "Who could give us permission to put up my poster?"

Her mother thought for a moment and said, "We would have to ask the mayor."

Shyloe shouted, "We're doers! Let's contact the mayor."

Her mother emailed Mayor Fetters that same day. Momma's fingers bounced across the laptop keys as they tap danced along.

The mayor said, "I'd like to meet Shyloe. Would you bring her to my office next week?"

One day that next week, her mother helped Shyloe comb her hair and find the right clothes to wear. Her Pap-Pap went, too. Some called him Pastor Bill, but Shyloe and Sara called him Pap-Pap. Shyloe, her mother and Pap-Pap gathered up her poster and carried it down to City Hall where the mayor's office was located. The large old city building standing on the corner looked like a castle protecting that part of town. The flag on top of the pointy roof flapped in the breeze.

"I'm happy to meet you, Shyloe," the mayor said. "I like your poster and the ideas you shared with me. Would you be able to come to the Huntington City Common Council meeting to present your poster?"

Shyloe was so excited she felt butterflies flit through her tummy. She wasn't sure she liked that feeling but she enjoyed meeting the mayor.

The mayor told her, "Cleaning up our beautiful city and keeping it clean has been part of the work of the City Council. They make laws about where to dump trash and how to keep our parks free from litter. You're a doer. I think they would like to hear what you have to say."

Shyloe thought about standing up in front of people and telling them about stinky garbage left in the park. A yummy banana left on a picnic table in the sun all day, would smell rotten by the next morning.

"Yes, I'd like to come to the city council meeting," Shyloe agreed. "I'm not sure what a city council is, but Momma and I can look it up and read about it before the meeting," Shyloe grinned. "I like to research about things."

She reached out to shake the mayor's hand because that's what grownups do. Mayor Fetter's hand was large and felt strong.

While visiting the mayor, someone took a picture of Shyloe with Mayor Fetters in front of a wall of pictures.

"Who are those men?" Shyloe asked.

Her Pap-Pap answered, "Those are pictures of all the men who have been mayor of Huntington, Indiana."

"But, there aren't any women up there," Shyloe noticed. She looked closely at the picture of the man with a monocle. A monocle is a round framed glass over only one eye. Shyloe tried not to giggle. She'd never seen anyone with only half a pair of glasses.

The next month the meeting was scheduled. Shyloe's mother explained what a City Council is. Momma said, "A City Council is a small group of people elected by the people in the community who make the rules for a city."

"What if I don't like one of the rules?" Shyloe asked.

Momma answered, "If a lot of people agree that it isn't a good rule or law, the Council can change the rule."

The afternoon of the meeting, Shyloe asked her mother to fix her hair and put the ends into curls. The comb pulled a little and made her eyes water. Still, she knew looking clean and neat would help people listen to her better. Then she put on her favorite dress and her good white shoes. She was very excited because she was going to be a good citizen and share her ideas with the City Council.

It was an important event for Shyloe. Her daddy, his mother Nana, and her husband came. Mimi came with Pap-Pap, too. They wanted her to know that she was doing an important thing. Being a doer and being a good citizen are things we all want to be.

When they got to the castle building, she was so thrilled she danced and twirled as she approached the door. When she saw one early lightening bug wink at her, she knew it would be a good evening.

At City Hall they all rode up to the third floor on the elevator. The doors closed and the elevator swooshed as it moved up.

The Council room was across the hall from the mayor's office. Shyloe recognized the room because Momma showed her where it was when they were there to meet the mayor. The old wooden floors squeaked as more people came to hear the business of the council.

A lady introduced herself to Shyloe and her mother. The lady said she worked for the newspaper and wanted to interview Shyloe. She asked the happy little citizen questions about her poster and Shyloe's thoughts on littering. Shyloe answered every question, even though she was getting more nervous about her talk.

Then the reporter took her picture. The flash of her camera made white spots bleep before Shyloe's eyes. The lady said she would use the answers to the questions and the picture she took in a story she would write for the local newspaper.

In the big council room the mayor began the meeting. He told the council members he had a guest who would talk to them before they began their business. He invited Shyloe to come to the microphone.

The funny desk was very tall. Shyloe had to stand on tiptoes and stretch her leg muscles as far as they could reach. Her mother brought a small step stool so Shyloe could reach the podium, which was a tall desk where she could put her papers.

Since Shyloe was six years old and wouldn't be seven for two more months, she wasn't tall enough to reach the microphone. She strained to stretch her neck up as much as she could, but the mic was still out of her reach. So, the mayor came down from his big desk and held the microphone for her. Shyloe had to stretch up as tall as possible on top of the step-stool, so she could talk into the mic. Suddenly, she felt her muscles groan and begin to cramp, like someone was tying a knot in her legs.

Quickly, she lowered her feet flat to the floor, then up again. The exercise coaxed her muscles to relax.

Mayor Fetters put her poster up on an easel for everyone to see. There were several people in the audience. Some had business with the council and some came to watch the city government as they worked. All seemed interested in what Shyloe had to say.

Shyloe had several ideas on her poster, *Don't Trash on Your Future*. When she began to read them, she felt giddy inside.

(1) An average person produces four and a half pounds of trash every day.
(2) It takes twenty years for one plastic bag to decompose.
(3) If all of the US recycled, it would generate a million and a half jobs nationwide.
(4) Recycling a single aluminum can saves enough electricity to power a TV for 3 hours.
(5) There is a patch of garbage in the Pacific Ocean that is two times the size of Texas.

Shyloe was nervous so her momma stood beside her and gently rubbed her back. Then Shyloe remembered a trick for overcoming that anxious feeling you get in the pit of your stomach. Rather than feeling icky blicky inside, Shyloe decided to become a doer. She said later, "When I felt like I might cry, I sang in my head."

Mimi said, "It's okay to be nervous. It's even okay to be so excited, bubbles feel like they're forming and you're afraid you'll cry. What's important is to continue to do what you really want to do. You sang to pop the bubbles. Good for you."

Shyloe wanted to tell them even more. She told the council, "When you clean up trash, wear gloves and wash your hands after. When you pick up trash, little bits of junk can still cause a problem."

Reading from her notes she added, "Trash can make water undrinkable. Drink tap water to cut out the use of plastic bottles." The more she talked, the more the nervous jitters began to settle down. "Be sure to cut up plastic rings that hold bottles in a package because ocean life can get caught in the circles. Also, don't buy things with lots of wrappers." She let out a big "whew" as the last of her anxiety blew away. "Oh, and be sure to recycle," she reminded everyone.

When she finished her talk, she wondered why people in the audience had their cell phones out. She didn't even know the people. When she realized they were taking her picture, her chest puffed up all by itself. As she watched the people smile at her, it made her feel good. She smiled back as the corners of her mouth jumped up. She guessed being a doer not a don'ter is important.

When Shyloe finished reading all of the important points about littering, she relaxed. Mayor Fetters asked Shyloe if it would be okay for the council members to ask her some questions. At first she wondered inside if she would know the answers.

She knew about littering. She didn't like it when she saw people leave things in the parks for others to smell, trip over, or pick up after them. She stood up tall and nodded. "Sure," she said.

Several of the members asked her about littering. Shyloe was glad to answer. One of them asked, "What do you want to be when you grow up?"

At first, Shyloe's eyes began to dance and sparkled. She thought for a minute and said she would like to be a teacher. She had wanted to be a teacher since she was in pre-school.

Mayor Fetters said, "Shyloe, we have something for you." He went back to his desk and picked up a round shiny thing with blue and red enamel on it. "Shyloe, we have an award to help you remember your special time here. You did a great job. It's a Leadership Medallion."

Shyloe had no idea they would give her a Medal. She could feel the pride the others shared with her.

The mayor held up the medallion for everyone to see. "It says, 'Leaders Solve Problems. We Serve Huntington.' The other side says, 'Leaders Serve People, City of Huntington, Indiana.'" Then he had Shyloe's picture taken with him, several council members, and the medal.

Finally the mayor said, "When you were in my office, you told me something else you'd like to be some day. Do you want to tell everyone what you told me?"

Shyloe's eyes brightened even more. Giggles floated up inside her. She knew she wanted to become a citizen doer. "I want to be the first female mayor of Huntington," she said. Everyone clapped for Shyloe, a leader, a problem solver, and a doer.

Teacher Suggestions

1. The children in your class could create their own poster on the theme of recycling. They can put their poster in their window as Shyloe did or take it to a friendly manager/owner for display at their business.

2. Your class could go on a field trip to a local recycling center. Discuss how to recycle in the classroom and what to expect at the center.

3. The class could take a field trip to City Hall, meet the mayor, and tour the room where the Common Council meets.

This is a true story about my granddaughter, Shyloe, and her meeting with Mayor Brooks Fetters. I have permission from the Mayor of Huntington to use his name in this book. He said, "Either Mayor Fetters or Mayor Brooks." Shyloe calls him Mayor Fetters.

Other Books by Dr. Doris Gaines Rapp

For advanced Middle Grade readers (the high-end of ages 8 to 13) and YA's (Young Adult level - age 12 to 18, and any readers above that who like a great read).

Escape from the Belfry	Hiawassee, Child of the Meadow
Escape from the Shadows	Smoke from Distant Fires
Lincoln's Christmas Mouse – a picture book	

For readers, YA and above, who love good books without violence, bad language or other elements that may offend some readers, check out books by Doris Gaines Rapp:

amazon.com	Crime Beat, She Blogged—The Return of Faith (2019)
barnesandnoble.com	Crime Beat, She Blogged—Just in Time (2019)
cokesbury.com	Length of Days – The Age of Silence
	Length of Days – Beyond the Valley of the Keepers
	Length of Days – Search for Freedom

About the Author…

Doris Gaines Rapp, Ph.D.

An author with additional interests and training, Doris Rapp is a psychologist, speaker, and former teacher. She has spoken at several writers' conferences and has directed the Counseling Centers at two universities. The last few years she has written full time. Books may be ordered from your bookstore or online: amazon.com, barnesandnoble.com. Her work with Prayer Therapy is posted on her blog: prayertherapyofjesus.blogspot.com. Select The Prayer Therapy of Jesus from Amazon or Barnes and Noble.

She and her husband have survived the rearing of six children. They live in Huntington, Indiana.

Website: dorisgainesrapp.com

www.ingramcontent.com/pod-product-compliance
Lightning Source LLC
Chambersburg PA
CBHW050855010526

44118CB00004BA/171